The First Gift of Christmas

The First Gift of Christmas

Richard Paul Evans

SALT LAKE CITY

First edition
99 98 97 96   10 9 8 7 6 5 4 3 2 1

This is a Peregrine Smith Book, published by
Gibbs Smith, Publisher
P.O. Box 667
Layton, Utah 84041

Design by J. Scott Knudsen, Park City, Utah

Manufactured in the United States of America

Library of Congress Cataloging-in-Publication Data
Evans, Richard Paul.
The first gift of Christmas / Richard Paul Evans.
   p.   cm.
   ISBN 0-87905-763-7
   1. Christian poetry, American. 2. Christmas—Poetry.
I. Title.
PS3555.V259F57   1996
811'.54—dc20   96-20657
                                        CIP

To Jenna,
  Allyson and
Abigail

CONTENTS

In Search of
Christmas

I was more amused than amazed when I read in the *New York Times* of a strange East-meets-West phenomenon. The Japanese have discovered Christmas and, no doubt aided by enterprising retailers, taken the season to heart. Aware that the holiday has something to do with an overfed man in a red suit and the birth of Jesus Christ, they, not unlike myself, don't quite grasp the connection. It should have come as no surprise when, last Christmas,

American tourists were horrified to encounter a Christmas display in a Tokyo department-store window with a red-suited Santa Claus nailed to a cross.

I'm afraid that I've crucified a few Santas myself.

As one who cherishes the season, I reluctantly confess to spending a good deal of my life oblivious to its deeper meaning—guilty of not seeing the forest for the Christmas trees. In defense of my ignorance, it is not difficult to be distracted by Yule tinsel, for Christmas is most often defined by its myriad symbols: stars, bells, wreaths, reindeer, baubles, bows, mistletoe, poinsettias, candles, and candy canes.

But when the candy-striped façade is stripped away, what is it that remains of the season?

It was in just such a circumstance that I truly learned of Christmas—in a place where there was no Christmas. A few years back, I spent a Christmas in Taiwan—a world removed from Rudolphs and Grinches, church bells and manger scenes—far from friends and family, far from the tinsel street-lamp ornaments and garlands that overhung the snow-packed streets of my home in Salt Lake City. Outwardly, there was no evidence of the season. None. But among the golden temples, water buffaloes and rice-hatted farmers, *Christmas was there, inside my heart*. And even though it made my heart burn with homesickness—*my heart did burn*. Brightly. And I was filled with love for the season and gratitude for all that I was missing: my family, my friends, my country. I was fortunate to have so much in my life to miss so badly.

In this state of heart, I came to the realization that it is, perhaps, not as much a question of what Christmas is about as it is what *we are about*. That is, while we are attempting to define the season, the season, in fact, is far more adept at defining us. For Christmas reveals us as it questions our hearts and intents and asks whether we will hear its call. If we choose to ignore its voice, it may die in our ears; but its resonant call remains, and we become as the deaf man who, in the midst of thunder, curses the silence.

THE FIRST GIFT OF CHRISTMAS is a collection of my thoughts and introspections on this magical season and the stages contained within—the *four seasons of Christmas*.

The first season of Christmas is the advent. "What Christmas Asks" is a rhyme about the symbolism behind the Christmas story as revealed in Luke 2.

The second season of Christmas is Christmas Eve. "The First Gift of Christmas" has obvious reference to my novel *The Christmas Box*. This poem is dedicated to my parents and is reminiscent of their love and sacrifice through the years.

The third season of Christmas is the anticipated morn. "Christmas Morning" is about a lesson contained in that rhapsodic dawn.

The fourth and final season of Christmas is Christmas night, the closure of the long-awaited day. "Is It Enough?" is a Christmas-night introspection. I love its message and was pleased when *Family Circle* magazine asked to include it in their December 1995 issue.

May these thoughts of Christmas's four seasons bestow upon you and those you love greater appreciation for the season, that we may all better hear what Christmas asks of us.

God bless us all to receive this joyous season.

Richard Paul Evans

THE
FIRST SEASON
OF
CHRISTMAS

The Advent

What

CHRISTMAS ASKS

(Luke 2)

Our family gathers 'round open script,

A Yule observance yearly kept,

And reads the lines of Bible writ,

The story that all year has slept.

A mother—Mary—in travail,

In search of place that she might birth,

That sin and heartbreak not prevail,

A son to bring into the earth.

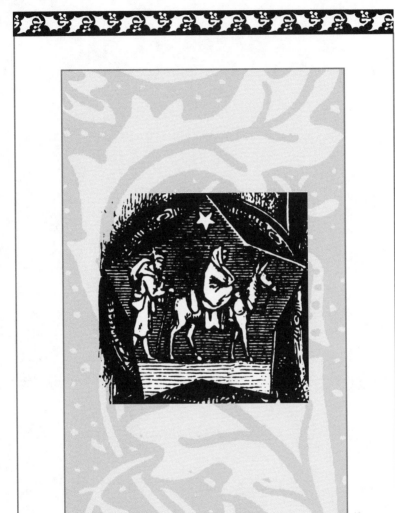

And as she crossed from door to door,

A stranger in unwelcomed place,

Rejection met with each implore

This small request from Heaven's face.

And we this night in our warm room,

Two thousand years removed and safe,

Condemn those who sent her away,

Claim we'd act different in their place.

And yet, we too must make this choice,

As Christmas moves from inn to inn,

If we will hear its gentle voice

And open up and let it in.

For Christmas yearly asks of us

The question that it must impart:

Will we grant access to our soul?

Or is there room within our heart?

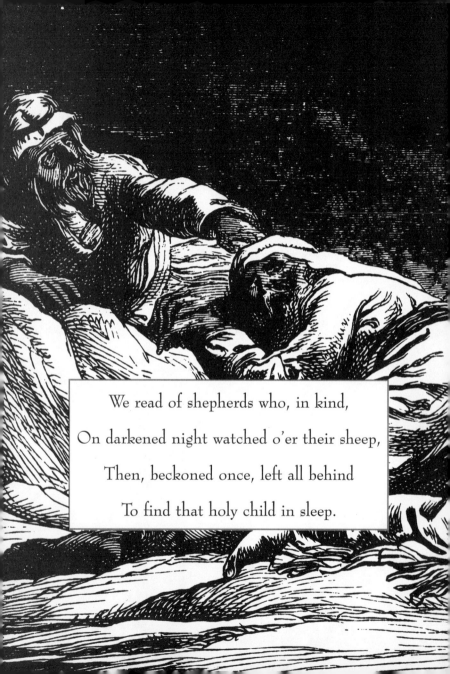

We read of shepherds who, in kind,

On darkened night watched o'er their sheep,

Then, beckoned once, left all behind

To find that holy child in sleep.

At Christmastime we, too, are called

To leave our troubled lives of care,

To set aside our burdened minds,

With God and man our hearts to share.

For Christmas yearly asks of us

That question sent on angel wings:

Is there still room within our heart

To leave our cares for loftier things?

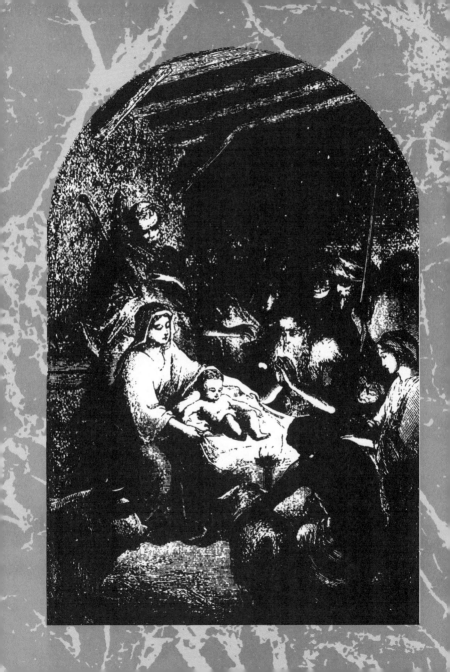

We read of wise men, traveled far,

Their gaze set on a bright new light

And lifted to exalted star,

Inspired by that celestial sight.

And Christmas too does ask of us

To raise our eyes to higher spheres,

Believe the best in life and man,

Embrace new hope, release our fears.

And so this scripture, read anew,

Was not just penned for days all past.

With each new year our hearts renew,

And this, of us, each Christmas asks.

THE
SECOND SEASON
OF
CHRISTMAS

The Eve

THE FIRST GIFT
OF CHRISTMAS

To my father and mother

Christmas Eve.

The snow collects in tranquil fells

As children retire in reticent slumber

And Christmas candles weep for

the end of their usefulness.

In the peace of the hour—

The gifts wrapped and marked,

Beneath lit boughs of fading pine—

I recline and sample a confection offering

Left for a saint by children of faith.

Through closing eyes,

The lights blur into an iridescent vision.

My thoughts span a chasm of time,

Accompanying my heart

To a scene of Christmas magic

From the hands of loving parents wrought—

Who somehow, some way, spun gold from flax

To deliver such treasures as childhood could dream;

Taught how to give with no thought of receipt

But the receiver's joy.

And in this deed,

The greater gift bestowed to their

children,

A legacy I treasure in my heart

And pass on to my own,

A symbol of a timeless offering

Bequeathed to earth millennia ago

At that first humble Christmas morn.

The first gift of Christmas—

A parent's love.

THE
THIRD SEASON
OF
CHRISTMAS

The Morning

CHRISTMAS MORNING

The long-awaited morning comes,

Precedes the sun

In children's eager wakenings.

A gilded tree

In quiet twilight shimmers,

Anticipates the dawn assault

Of flannel-clad children

Frantically descending

To scavenge its boughs

In search of treasure.

And now,

The season's slow climax reached,

Proclaimed by tattered paper and empty boxes

Tossed asunder in festive abandon,

Their secret contents compromised,

Revealed in joyful caches.

Somewhere in the morning dawn,

A threshhold of the season crossed,

As what to be is now what was.

And to the mind a thought inspires:

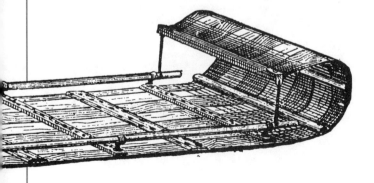

Each empty box confirms anew

A lesson best learned and taken to heart,

The wanting is often better than that hoped for,

The journey better than the destination.

And, ponderous, in thought I find

This great truth to be good and right,

For life, like Christmas, is but a journey,

And we, its children,

Were born as travelers.

THE
FOURTH SEASON
OF
CHRISTMAS

The Night

IS IT ENOUGH?

Christmas Night.

As the evening falls

like the curtain on a

long-awaited show,

I hold my daughter,

just one last time

this season,

In the warm bath of the

Christmas-tree lights.

And I wonder.

Did the Yuletide parties
and gatherings fill her
with a sense of family?

Did the Christmas rituals
unite her in a shared
commonality with
her fellowmen?

Did the music of Christmas

heal her of a cynical world

and inspire her with hopes

of something greater?

Did the gifts she shared

teach her that the greatest gifts

are received in the giving?

Did the once-wrapped

presents of Christmas remind

her of a greater gift given

many Christmases ago?

And I wonder.

Is there enough awe

in my child,

enough magic left,

to save a world?

For within my heart

I lament a great truth—

That the only

promise of childhood

is that it will end.

And I wonder what

I have given her

to take its place.

And is it enough?